# What's Behind the Blue Door?

## CREATIVE WRITING PROMPTS
to Invite Inspiration

By WriteGirl

CHRONICLE BOOKS
SAN FRANCISCO

ISBN 978-1-7972-1973-8

Manufactured in China.
Design by Jonathan Glick.
Illustrations by Jonathan Glick.
Typeset in YWFT Neighborhood and Caitiff.

10 9 8 7 6 5 4 3 2 1

A portion of the proceeds from the sale of this journal will
benefit WriteGirl, a creative writing and mentoring organization.
Learn more at www.writegirl.org.

Chronicle Books LLC
680 Second Street
San Francisco, California 94107
www.chroniclebooks.com

"Believe in the worth of your own unique voice."

—Amanda Gorman

WriteGirl Alum
Inaugural Poet
*New York Times* Bestselling Author
National Youth Poet Laureate

# INTRODUCTION
## By Keren Taylor

*We write to understand, we write to communicate, we write to protest, and we write to entertain.*

Writing is a window to what lies within and all that is going on around us, but it can be hard to know where to start. Well . . . start here! This journal is for anyone who wants to write and is looking for inspiration. Winding through these pages, you'll find dozens of writing activities, tips, and strategies for tapping into your creative ideas and moving beyond the blank page.

For over twenty years, I have been producing workshops, events, and publications that inspire young women to write their personal stories, poetry, fiction, scenes, and songs. I founded WriteGirl to offer a different kind of writing workshop—an environment where you are surrounded by positive support and flooded with evocative questions and activities specifically designed to spark your imagination and unlock your creative voice. The WriteGirl philosophy and approach are all about opening the door so you can connect to the utterly unique and creative ideas within you. We put this journal together to offer you that same experience, with motivation on nearly every page and plenty of open space for you to write.

My own bookshelves are brimming with well-worn journals filled with my thoughts, feelings, poetry, and stories. Writing helps me reflect on where I've come from, and it also allows me to understand where I am now and where I want to go next. Writing is the one way I can puzzle through the messiness of life and find my way forward toward the life of purpose and joy that I seek.

Take this journal with you throughout your day, and let it ignite your inner writer as it guides you to write about yourself and the world around you. Start at the first page and keep going to the end, or just open randomly to any page and start there! Write every day, or just on Sundays. Write in a café, in a park, in a waiting room, or on an airplane. Write in any form, such as a list, poem, story, essay, or simply a torrent of words. Try all the activities and see which ones really get your pen moving. Feel free to skip an activity or modify it to adapt to whatever mood, memories, or moment you find yourself in.

Take a deep breath and turn the page.

Your creative journey starts now.

There is a bright blue door. You go through it.

What happens?

Adonis had been working at bookstore for three years now, and in that time had learned alot about its customers. You had the standerd ~~busines~~ office workers coming in on their lunch breaks, the, but every so often a new face would come in.

WRITE AND YOU WILL ALWAYS BE HEARD!

You are standing at the edge of the ocean, and a bottle washes up at your feet. Inside, there is an urgent message for you. What is it?

Finish this sentence: What you don't know about me is . . .

WRITE ABOUT WHAT MAKES YOU CURIOUS!

Somewhere on this page, write a small secret message to yourself with some positive advice that you find personally inspiring or calming.

HE ONLY MAGIC TO WRITING IS TO
IT YOURSELF DOWN AND DO IT.

Our moods can be like weather patterns inside us.

Write about what the weather is like inside you right now.

Afraid of the blank page? Scribble all over this page for one minute without stopping.

What you collect in your backpack, pocket, or purse  says a lot about you—old receipts, menus, bus ticket stubs, phone numbers, and lists are all documentation of where you have been or plan to go. Take out a few items and place them in front of you. Examine them and see what they reveal about your identity, hopes, and fears. Identify one or more of the objects and write the first story that comes to mind.

WRITE YOUR
FIRST DRAFT
SO QUICKLY
THAT YOUR
INNER CRITIC
CAN'T KEEP UP.

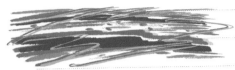

You smell freshly cut grass.

Where are you? Who is there?

STORY ONLY YOU CAN TELL.

There's someone you need to say something to. If you were to sit down and write them a letter right now, who would you be writing to? What do you want to tell this person? You don't need to mail it to them . . . but you can if you want to.

Write about a memory involving water.

Write in your pajamas at midnight.

START WITH SOMETHING TRUE

Randomly select five to ten words from your mail, a shampoo bottle label, or a book. Write each word on a separate slip of paper. Toss the words on a table and mix up the pile. Use some (or all!) of the words to write a poem or story about yourself.

You picked up the wrong suitcase. What's in it?

Describe the character that is the opposite of you.

REATE LIKE AN

RCHITECT CREATES

JILDINGS—START

TH A BLUEPRINT.

Find a photograph. Spend some time with it and notice all the details. Get lost in it. Then start writing. Write about what you see or don't see.

_TAKE IT UP A NOTCH:_ Write about what might have happened next, right after the photo was taken.

POETRY IS FEELING THE EVERYDAY AROUND YOU—BATHE IN IT.

Every person's body is unique—what's unique about yours?
Write about it.

*TAKE IT UP A NOTCH:* Make it into a superpower.

NOT IN THE MOOD TO WRITE? WRITE ANYWAY AND LET YOUR EMOTIONS COME OUT ON THE PAGE.

Set a timer or watch the clock. Take five minutes to write a complete fictional story. Include conflict, resolution, and at least one number and one color. Go!

TAKE THE JOURNEY WITH YOUR CHARACTERS. DON'T BE AFRAID TO TALK TO THEM.

# WRITE THE ENDING FIRST.

You've found a wallet. What's in it?

Create the character it belongs to

and the story of how they lost it.

# THEN CREATE THE STORY.

NEVER WRITE ON AN EMPTY STOMACH.

Play a song that inspires a nostalgic mood.

Write without stopping until the song ends.

OTHERS. WRITE TO INSPIRE OTHERS.

Use a sense other than sight to tell a personal story
about a place where something special happened.

TAKE YOUR STORY IDEA

FOR A WALK AROUND

THE BLOCK. LET THE

TREES, FLOWERS, AND

YOUR NEIGHBOR'S DOG

INSPIRE YOU.

Pick a random word, and write the first sentence of a story with it in mind. Then just keep going!

Pick a color. List as many things that are that color as
you can fit on this page, then write a poem mentioning
at least three of those things.

WRITING IS PORTABLE. TAKE YOURSELF SOMEWHERE NEW, AND LET THE VIEW INSPIRE YOUR WORDS.

Translate your poem into another language, then translate it back to English. See what changes.

EVEN WHEN YOU DON'T

FEEL LIKE WRITING,

WRITE! YOU CAN EVEN

WRITE ABOUT HOW YOU

DON'T FEEL LIKE WRITING.

Write as fast and as much as you can on this page, without editing or concern for logic or grammar.

THE TIME TO WRITE IS NOW.

A building or house can be inspiration for writing.

Take a walk and see which buildings speak to you.

# USE DETAIL WHEN WRITING: WRITE ABOUT THE MISSING BUTTON, THE HAIR OUT OF PLACE, THE GLANCE YOU SAW THEM THROW.

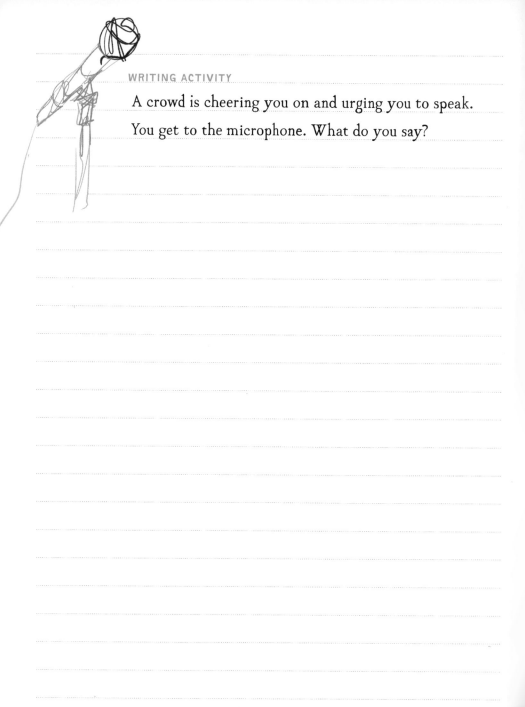

A crowd is cheering you on and urging you to speak.
You get to the microphone. What do you say?

YOU JUST HAVE TO **WRITE** TODAY.

Write equal parts of what you do and don't know about the ocean.

YOUR FIRST DRAFT IS LIKE PLACING A

LUMP OF CLAY ONTO A POTTERY WHEEL.

IT'S NOT SUPPOSED TO LOOK LIKE A

POT YET. IT TURNS INTO THE FINISHED

PIECE AS YOU SHAPE IT AND REWRITE.

Sometimes writing inspiration comes from unexpected places. Find an interesting sentence from a text in your phone. Use that as the first line in a poem or story. Don't be afraid of something that seems completely improbable—that's where the fun is!

Select three objects you can see around you right now.
Imagine they are clues to a mystery. Write that story.

TAKE YOUR JOURNAL TO A PLACE YOU HAVE NEVER
BEEN BEFORE. NEW PLACES CAN BRING OUT NEW IDEAS.

# WRITE FOR YOURSELF FIRST. DON'T WORRY ABOUT

WRITING ACTIVITY

Your shoes carry you through your world. They have been with you to public events and private moments. What would your shoes say if they could talk? What have they seen? Select a pair of your shoes and write through their perspective. It can be helpful to pick up the shoes and really examine them. (If nothing flows, try a different pair of shoes— some have more stories than others!)

# WHAT PEOPLE WILL THINK OF YOUR WRITING.

You have a magic eraser to use on anything in the world.

What will you erase?

Write about your name. It can be your first name, last name, middle name, or nickname, a name you were almost called, or a name you wish you were or weren't called. We all have powerful feelings about our name. What does your name mean to you?

HELLO
my name is

What would you call yourself if you
could give yourself a new name?

Write a dialogue between two characters.
Listen to your characters. Let them tell you
the story.

LET YOUR COPY COOL. LEAVE

YOUR WRITING ALONE FOR A

FEW DAYS, OVERNIGHT, OR AT

LEAST AN HOUR. WHEN YOU

RETURN TO IT,

YOU'LL BRING A

FRESH PERSPECTIVE.

Think about a family member or friend you love. Write about how they walk, gesture, or laugh, or about the kinds of things they say to you. Use all your senses! As you write, think about any sounds, scents, or textures that come to mind.

*TAKE IT UP A NOTCH:* Write up a complete sensory description of this person.

# YOU HAVE STORIES TO TELL.

TAKE THE TIME TO WRITE THEM DOWN.

Invent a new flower or plant. Draw it; name it; write about where it grows and how people interact with it.

WRITING ACTIVITY

In a waiting room or line? Write down snippets of dialogue you can hear around you. Later, use these snippets to invent characters and create a scene. When writing dialogue, give each character a distinct voice so the reader knows immediately who is speaking.

Write about your life in headlines only. First, give your newspaper a name. Then, write headlines for every section of your life's newspaper. What headline do you put at the top? What order do you put them in? Add a few more to complete this newspaper of you.

Finish this sentence: I'm fired up about . . .

DON'T HAVE TIME TO WRITE? JUST TAKE SIXTY SECONDS AND SEE WHAT LANDS ON THE PAGE.

Write an ode. Odes can be written for heroes and leaders, underdogs and outcasts. You can even write an ode to an object, such as flip-flops or a storage closet. Select a person or object that you would like to highlight with a tribute poem.

You're shaping a world with your pen. Who do you want
to see represented in this world? Who might you
want to leave out? Who do you want to highlight?

TRY WRITING IN DIFFERENT

PLACES—ON A BENCH IN

A PARK, AT THE TOP OF

SOME STAIRS, OR AT A

BUS STOP—AND SEE HOW

IT CHANGES YOUR IDEAS.

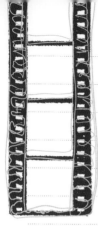

Write the voice-over script for a movie trailer
about something unusual that happened to
you or that you wish would happen to you.
Write in short, dramatic phrases.

Write a poem that incorporates earth, air, water, and fire.

ET THE PEN CONVEY YOUR JOY,

HAME, LONGING, PAIN, AND

MOTIONS. LET THOSE EMOTIONS

REATHE IN YOUR STORY.

Choose a different writing instrument than you usually use, such as a crayon or marker. Write in a spiral, upside down, around the edges, in HUGE or tiny letters.

Don't worry about straight lines or crossing your T's. Just let yourself write!

See how your writing changes when you switch things up.

Pick a specific or unusual profession—taxidermist, pancake flipper, ice sculptor—and write a first-person account of a particularly eventful day at work.

A list poem is just that: a list of things, any things, and the more detailed the list, the better. Try writing a list poem based on things that make you smile, things to do when you can't sleep, things that are square, things that are hot, things that are mysterious, or sounds you love.

Write a story about the people you see daily but have never talked to.

WRITE AT NIGHT. SOME IDEAS ARRIVE
AFTER A FULL DAY OF LIVING.

Imagine waking up in the morning as an animal. What
kind of animal are you? Write a story about how you
go about your day as this animal. Write about how your
family and friends react.

*TAKE IT UP A NOTCH:* Put a journal next to your bed and record what kind of animal you feel like every morning for a week, and why. How do your notes change from day to day? What kind of animal do you feel like before you go to sleep at night? Is it the same as in the morning?

See if you can write one long run-on sentence, without stopping, for five minutes. Just let the words flow.

ALWAYS KEEP A

PENCIL OR PEN

WITH SOME PAPER

NEXT TO YOUR BED

BECAUSE WHEN

YOU HAVE AN IDEA

WORTH WRITING

DOWN, WHO

NEEDS SLEEP?!

Open your journal and write down everything
that comes to you for the next five minutes.
You might find yourself continually jumping to
new thoughts, or you might find that there's
one topic on your mind. Keep your pen moving.

*TAKE IT UP A NOTCH:* Try doing this every day at the same time (when you wake up, immediately after dinner, etc.) for at least seven days. Every writer needs a routine.

Imagine you are at the top of a mountain looking out and seeing the entirety of something. What do you see? How do you feel?

Compare someone who inspires you to an object, event, or place in your everyday life. Think of both physical and metaphorical objects. Give details about how they are the same and how they are different.

*TAKE IT UP A NOTCH:* Try different objects for
the same person to see which fits best.

HEN YOU SIT DOWN TO WRITE SO YOU CAN GET INTO A CREATIVE MOOD.

Close your eyes for one minute and take in all the
nonvisual stimuli. Now write a poem about what you
just experienced—the way your breath feels moving
through your body, the conversation you just overheard, the way the
scent of fresh coffee wafts past. Write about all the things you notice.

Give yourself word limits. For example, write a poem about the last time you laughed or cried really hard, using only five lines and five words per line. Or write a short story in just ten sentences. Sometimes freedom can come from restriction.

UT WHATEVER IS NOT WORKING. BE BRAVE.

HE THING ABOUT REVISION IS THAT NOBODY

KES IT, BUT EVERYBODY NEEDS IT.

Look around you right now. Choose two objects that seem totally unrelated. Put them on a table near you. Start writing and find a way to incorporate each of the items as you tell a story or create a poem.

Where is home for you? It could be a building, a state of mind, a gathering of people, a landscape, or a feeling that comes over you. Write about what home means to you.

LEARN SOMETHING. TRAVEL. TALK
TO STRANGERS. FALL IN LOVE.
GET YOUR HEART BROKEN. HAVE
EXPERIENCES. CONNECT WITH
OTHERS. THE MORE YOU KNOW
ABOUT THE WORLD, THE MORE
YOU HAVE TO WRITE ABOUT.

In writing, repetition is used in many ways. It creates texture and rhythm. It emphasizes an important thought or evokes a particular mood. Create a poem or story in which you repeat a word or phrase to drive your point home.

WRITE WHEN YOU HAVE A STRONG EMOTION SURGING WITHIN YOU

Pick a place that you love to visit, and make a list of the sensory details you find there. Maybe it's the feel and taste of gauzy, pink cotton candy at a carnival; the crackle of leaves beneath your shoes in a forest; or the salty scent of the ocean.

*TAKE IT UP A NOTCH:* Weave the details together to create a poem.

START FROM THE END AND WO

Describe one aspect of your culture: a special food you enjoy with your family or a place or event that is meaningful to you.

*TAKE IT UP A NOTCH:* Describe five more moments, places, events, or activities that reflect your culture or identity.

DING SPECIFIC NAMES IN YOUR WORK

LPS YOUR WRITING COME ALIVE. FOR

AMPLE, IF YOUR WRITING INCLUDES

GROCERY STORE OR A MUSEUM, GIVE

A NAME LIKE "MAXINE'S GENERAL

ORE" OR "MUSEUM OF ROUNDNESS."

YOU WRITE A TREE INTO YOUR WORK,

T THE READER KNOW IF IT IS AN

K, MIMOSA, OR BLUE SPRUCE.

There is a strong link between color and emotion. Write about a color that you enjoy in your home, in your closet, or in your neighborhood. Write about that color from your perspective, and describe how it makes you feel.

Words matter. They can inspire people, influence politics, introduce new ideas, and even change the world. Write a letter or speech to a specific group of people, like all the artists, chefs, teachers, or women of the world. What does this group need to hear from you right now?

WHEN YOU WRITE, YOU INSPIRE THOSE WHO DON'T.

Write a page of questions beginning with "**WHAT iF?**"

Can a grocery list be poetry? Absolutely—just do a bit of tinkering. "Eggs, bread, milk, cat food" is not much of a poem, but add some detail—"eggs for deviling, that thick bread I ate at that bakery on Pearl Street"—and you're on your way. Create a poem out of your last grocery list.

EVERY STORY HAS A BEGINNING, MIDDLE, AND END.
THE CONFLICT ALONG THE WAY IS WHAT MAKES IT INTERESTING.

Imagine you are watching a sunrise. You are gaining strength, getting warmed up, and getting ready for something. Write about that!

ONE FORM OF EDITING IS READING YOUR WORDS OUT LOUD. YOU WILL HEAR WHAT YOU MIGHT NEED TO CHANGE, DELETE, OR ADD.

Continue the sentence "I am the person who . . . " as a way of
exploring your identity. Feel free to repeat the phrase. Go back in
time to yesterday or to many years ago. Write about things you
believe. Write about things you have done.

Many writers struggle when faced with a blank page. But your pen will fly across the page when you write about things that lift your emotions. Write a poem about something you love to do—it could be a sport, hobby, or Sunday morning routine. Describe why you love that activity, and include any insider words or phrases that are specific to that sport or activity.

ALWAYS LISTEN TO YOUR INTUITION WHEN WRITING. IF THERE IS SOMETHING THAT YOU LOVE IN YOUR WORK, DEFEND IT WITH ALL YOUR MIGHT.

If you could design a mural for your neighborhood,
what would be in the picture?

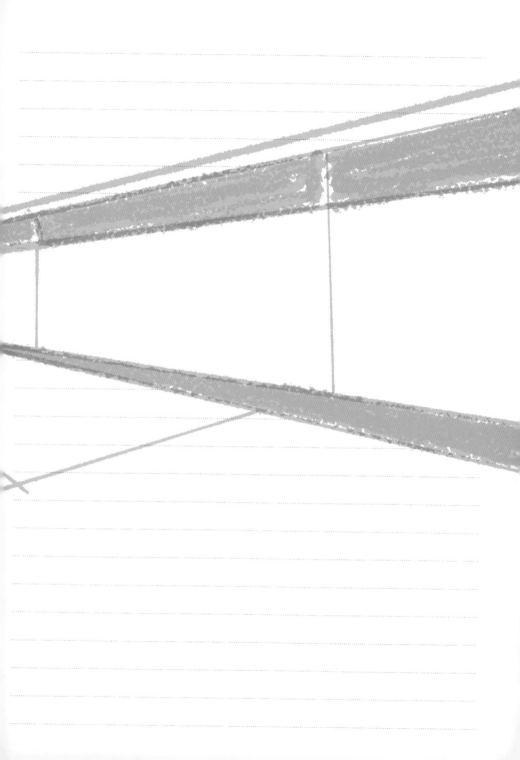

Think about a time when your feelings changed. Maybe you were lonely and then became calm; perhaps you were excited, then became frustrated. What were some of the steps that made that transition happen? Write about how you went through that change.

Write about a story that takes place at the intersection of two roads.
What happens there?

WRITE THE EMOTION THAT'S UNDER THE
SURFACE. GO DEEPER, LIKE YOU'RE DIVING
INTO THE DEEPEST PART OF THE SEA.

What everyday objects do you often touch or use, but take for granted? Select an object from your life—maybe it's your toothbrush or a drinking glass—and imagine all the ways this object might be seen as unique or captivating.

TAKE IT UP A NOTCH: What's the story that
has yet to be told about your object?

Envision a long hallway or tunnel. Imagine that stepping through this passageway will transform you in some way. Write about walking through this passage and who you become when you arrive on the other side.

WRITE THE STORY THAT FOLLOWS YOU: THE ONE THAT POPS INTO YOUR HEAD AT THE GROCERY STORE, WHILE WALKING THE DOG, OR JUST BEFORE YOU FALL ASLEEP.

Word association and brainstorming can surprise us with the ideas and images that come from these activities. Place a simple word like "tree" or "shadow" in the center of your journal page. What does the word make you think of? Write whatever comes to mind. Look at what you've written, and then consider where it takes you next. Avoid writing in straight lines. Just continue adding thoughts, words, and ideas randomly all around the page, like a cloud.

*TAKE IT UP A NOTCH:* On a new page, begin a poem by using some of the words, phrases, and ideas from your word-association experiment.

The newspaper can be a rich source of words, phrases, and stories. Select ten phrases or individual words that you are drawn to. Use a highlighter, or cut them right out of the paper with scissors. Now incorporate all ten words or phrases into a ten-line poem.

Life's special moments can be grand, like celebrating a graduation, or simple, like watching a sunset with a good friend. Make a list of a few standout moments from your own life, then close your eyes and really picture just one of them. Who is there? What does it smell, sound, and look like? How do you feel? Write a short prose poem about this moment. Try to describe how you feel without using the actual name of your feeling. *Show* the reader how you feel.

# CONVEY ENERGY IN YOUR WRITING

WITH WORDS THAT POP.

A large envelope was slipped under your door.

What message or clue do you find inside?

At WriteGirl, we wrap up every workshop by sharing something we liked, learned, or loved about the session. We call them "threads" because they are individual reflections that connect us all. Write something you liked, learned, or loved today. You might be surprised at what this reflection reveals!

DRAFT THE PLOT BEFORE
WRITING. IT KEEPS YOU
FROM GETTING LOST MIDWAY
THROUGH THE STORY.

TOO MANY DISTRACTIONS? INSTEAD OF TRYING TO IGNORE
THEM, WRITE ABOUT THEM. GET INTO THE SOUNDS, SMELLS,
TASTES, SIGHTS, FEELINGS, PEOPLE, OR THINGS THAT ARE
STEALING YOUR ATTENTION AND DRIVING YOU TO DISTRACTION.
PLACE THEM AT THE CENTER OF YOUR WRITING.